Born in 1971

By

Kerry Butters.

Born in 1971.

Millennium: 2nd millennium

Centuries: 19th century – **20th century** – 21st century

Decades: 1940s 1950s 1960s – **1970s** – 1980s 1990s 2000s

Years: 1968 1969 1970 – **1971** – 1972 1973 1974

1971 (MCMLXXI) was a common year starting on Friday (dominical letter C) of the Gregorian calendar, the 1971st year of the Common Era (CE) and *Anno Domini* (AD) designations, the 971st year of the 2nd millennium, the 71st year of the 20th century, and the 2nd year of the 1970s decade.

The world population increased by 2.1% this year; the highest in history.

Contents

Events

January

- January 2
    - Ibrox disaster: A stairway crush at the Rangers vs. Celtic football match in Glasgow, Scotland kills 66.
    - A ban on radio and television cigarette advertisements goes into effect in the United States.
- January 3 – BBC Open University begins in the United Kingdom.
- January 5 – The 1st ever ODI cricket match is played between Australia & England at the M.C.G.
- January 8 – Tupamaros kidnap Geoffrey Jackson, British ambassador to Uruguay, in Montevideo, keeping him captive until September.
- January 9 – Uruguayan president Jorge Pacheco Areco demands emergency powers for 90 days due to kidnappings, and receives them the next day.
- January 12 – The landmark television sitcom *All in the Family*, starring Carroll O'Connor as Archie Bunker, debuts on CBS.

- January 14 – Seventy Brazilian political prisoners are released in Santiago, Chile; Giovanni Enrico Bucher is released January 16.
- January 15 – The Aswan High Dam officially opens in Egypt.
- January 18 – Strikes in Poland demand the resignation of Interior Minister Kazimierz Switala. He resigns January 23 and is replaced by Franciszek Szlachcic.
- January 19 – Representatives of 23 western oil companies begin negotiations with OPEC in Tehran to stabilize oil prices; February 14 they sign a treaty with 6 Khalij el-Arab countries.
- January 24 – The Guinean government sentences to death 92 Guineans who helped Portuguese troops in the failed landing attempts in November 1970; 72 are sentenced to hard labor for life; 58 of the sentenced are hanged the next day.
- January 25
  - In Uganda, Idi Amin deposes Milton Obote in a coup, and becomes president.
  - In Los Angeles, Charles Manson and 3 female "Family" members are found guilty of the 1969 Tate–LaBianca murders.
  - Himachal Pradesh becomes the 18th Indian state.
  - *Intelsat IV* (F2) is launched; it enters commercial service over the Atlantic Ocean March 26.
- January 31 – Apollo program: *Apollo 14* (carrying astronauts Alan Shepard, Stuart Roosa, and Edgar Mitchell) lifts off on the third successful lunar landing mission.

January 15: Aswan Dam opens in Egypt.

February

- February 4 – In Britain, Rolls-Royce goes bankrupt and is nationalised.
- February 5 – *Apollo 14* lands on the Moon.
- February 7
  - An earthquake in the city of Tuscania, Italy kills 31.
  - Switzerland gives women voting rights in state elections, but not in all canton-specific ones.
  - Władysław Gomułka is expelled from the Central Council of the Polish Communist Party.
- February 8 – A new stock market index called the Nasdaq Composite debuts.
- February 9
  - The 6.5–6.7 Mw Sylmar earthquake hits the Greater Los Angeles Area with a maximum Mercalli intensity of XI (*Extreme*), killing 64 and injuring 2,000.
  - Satchel Paige becomes the first Negro League player to become voted into the Baseball Hall of Fame from the Negro League (Jackie Robinson was inducted July 23, 1962.)

- ○ Apollo program: *Apollo 14* returns to Earth after the third manned Moon landing.
- February 11 – The US, UK, USSR and others sign the Seabed Treaty, outlawing nuclear weapons on the ocean floor.
- February 11–February 12 – Palestinian and Jordanian fighters clash in Amman.
- February 13 – Vietnam War: Backed by American air and artillery support, South Vietnamese troops invade Laos.
- February 15
  - ○ Decimal Day: – The United Kingdom and Ireland both switch to decimal currency (see also decimalisation).
  - ○ Protesting Belgian farmers bring 3 live cows to crash the EEC meeting in Brussels.
- February 16 – In Italy, a local parliament elects the city of Catanzaro as the capital of Calabria; residents of Reggio di Calabria riot for 5 days because of the decision.
- February 20
  - ○ Fifty tornadoes rage in Mississippi, killing 74 people.
  - ○ The U.S. Emergency Broadcast System sends an erroneous warning, meant to be a standard weekly test conducted by NORAD in Cheyenne Mountain in Colorado; many radio stations just ignore it. The most notorious warning was of WOWO (AM) in Fort Wayne, Indiana.
- February 21 – The Convention on Psychotropic Substances is signed at Vienna.
- February 26 – Secretary General U Thant signs the United Nations proclamation of the vernal equinox as Earth Day.

- February 27 – Doctors in the first Dutch abortion clinic (Mildredhuis in Arnhem) start to perform abortus provocatus.
- February 28 – Evel Knievel sets a world record and jumps 19 cars in Ontario, California.

February 20: Tornadoes kill 74 in Mississippi.

February 5: Apollo 14 on Moon

February 7: Earthquake kills 31 in Tuscania, Italy.

March

- March 1
    - A bomb explodes in the men's room at the United States Capitol; the Weather Underground claims responsibility.
    - Pakistani President Agha Muhammad Yahya Khan indefinitely postpones the pending National Assembly session, precipitating massive civil disobedience in East Pakistan.
    - Canadian John Robarts ends his term of office as the 17th Premier of Ontario.
- March 4 – The southern part of Quebec, and especially Montreal, receive 16½" (42 cm) of snow in what becomes known as the Century's Snowstorm (*la tempête du siècle*).
- March 5 – The Pakistani army occupies East Pakistan.
- March 6 – A fire in a mental hospital at Burghölzli, Switzerland, kills 28 people.
- March 7
    - The British postal workers' strike, led by UPW General Secretary Tom Jackson, ends after 47 days.

- Sheikh Mujibur Rahman, political leader of then East Pakistan (present day-Bangladesh), delivers his famous speech in the Racecourse Field in Dhaka, calling on the masses to be prepared to fight for national independence.
- March 8
    - The Citizens' Commission to Investigate the FBI breaks into the Media, Pennsylvania offices of the Federal Bureau of Investigation and removes all the files.
    - 'Fight of the Century': Boxer Joe Frazier defeats Muhammad Ali at Madison Square Garden.
- March 12 – Hafez al-Assad becomes president of Syria.
- March 12–March 13 – The Allman Brothers Band plays their legendary concert at the Fillmore East.
- March 16 – Trygve Bratteli forms a government in Norway.
- March 18 – A landslide at Chungar, Peru crashes into Yanawayin Lake, killing 200.
- March 23 – General Alejandro Lanusse of Argentina takes power in a military coup.
- March 25 – The Pakistani army starts Operation Searchlight in East Pakistan from midnight, after President Agha Muhammad Yahya Khan, a military ruler, voids election results that gave the Awami League an overwhelming majority in the parliament.
- March 26
    - East Pakistan (now Bangladesh) independence is declared by Sheikh Mujibur Rahman and transmitted using East Pakistan Rifles (now Border Guards Bangladesh) radio.

- Nihat Erim (a former CHP member) forms the new government of Turkey (33rd government,composed mostly of technocrats).
- March 27 – East Pakistan (now Bangladesh) independence is repeatedly declared by Army Major (later President of Bangladesh) Ziaur Rahman on behalf of Sheikh Mujibur Rahman from Kalurghat Radio Station, Chittagong.
- March 28 – *The Ed Sullivan Show* airs its final episode.
- March 29
    - U.S. Army Lieutenant William Calley is found guilty of 22 murders in the My Lai Massacre and sentenced to life in prison (he is later pardoned).
    - A Los Angeles jury recommends the death penalty for Charles Manson and 3 female followers.

April

- April 1 – The United Kingdom lifts all restrictions on gold ownership.
- April 5
    - In Ceylon, a group calling themselves the People's Liberation Front begins a rebellion against the Bandaranaike government.
    - Chile and East Germany establish diplomatic relations.
    - Mount Etna erupts in Sicily.
- April 7 – Greece releases 261 political prisoners, 50 of whom are sent into internal exile.
- April 8 – A right-wing coup attempt is exposed in Laos.

- April 9 – Charles Manson is sentenced to death; in 1972, the sentence for all California Death Row inmates is commuted to life imprisonment.
- April 12 – Palestinians retreat from Amman to the north of Jordan.
- April 17
  - The People's Republic of Bangladesh forms, under Sheikh Mujibur Rahman, at Mujibnagor.
  - Libya, Syria and Egypt sign an agreement to form a confederation.
- April 19
  - The government of Bangladesh flees to India.
  - Sierra Leone becomes a republic.
  - The Soviet Union launches *Salyut 1*.
  - Followers of Charles Manson, the Manson Family, are sentenced to the gas chamber.
- April 20
  - *Swann v. Charlotte-Mecklenburg Board of Education*: The Supreme Court of the United States rules unanimously that busing of students may be ordered to achieve racial desegregation.
  - Cambodian Prime Minister Lon Nol resigns, but remains effectively in power until the next elections.
- April 21
  - Siaka Stevens is elected the first president of Sierra Leone.
  - François Duvalier, president of Haiti, dies; his son Jean-Claude Duvalier follows him as president-for-life.
- April 24
  - *Soyuz 10* docks with *Salyut 1*.

- Five hundred thousand people in Washington, D.C. and 125,000 in San Francisco march in protest against the Vietnam War.
  - A tsunami 85 m high rises over the Ryukyu Islands in Japan. It throws a 750-ton block of coral 2.5 km inland.
- April 25
  - Todor Zhivkov is re-elected as the leader of the Bulgarian Communist Party.
  - Franz Jonas is re-elected as president of Austria.
- April 26 – The government of Turkey declares a state of siege in 11 provinces, Ankara included, due to violent demonstrations.
- April 28 – The first number of *Il Manifesto* is issued in Italy.
- April 29 – Bolivia nationalizes the American-owned Matilde zinc mine.
- April 30 – The Milwaukee Bucks win the NBA World Championship, sweeping the Baltimore Bullets in 4 straight games.

May

- May 1
  - Amtrak begins inter-city rail passenger service in the United States.
  - The Ceylonese government promises amnesty for those guerillas who surrender before April 5.
- May 2 – In Ceylon, left-wing guerillas launch a series of assaults against public buildings.

- May 3
    - Arsenal F.C. wins the English Division 1 football league championship at the home of their bitter rivals, Tottenham Hotspur, with Ray Kennedy scoring the winner. (Arsenal FC will go on to win the league and cup 'double' 6 days later by defeating Liverpool in the FA Cup final).
    - The Harris Poll claims that 60% of Americans are against the Vietnam War.
    - East German leader Walter Ulbricht resigns as Communist Party leader but retains the position of head of state.
    - 1971 May Day Protests: Anti-war militants attempt to disrupt government business in Washington, D.C.; police and military units arrest as many as 12,000, most of whom are later released.
- May 5 – The US dollar floods the European currency markets and threatens especially the Deutsche Mark; the central banks of Austria, Belgium, Netherlands and Switzerland stop the currency trading.
- May 6 – The Ceylon government begins a major offensive against the People's Liberation Front.
- May 9
    - Arsenal FC beats Liverpool F.C. 2-1 to win the English FA Cup, thus completing the league and cup 'double'.
    - Mariner 8 fails to launch.
- May 12 – An earthquake in Turkey destroys most of the city of Burdur.
- May 15 – Efraim Elrom, Israeli ambassador to Turkey, is kidnapped; he is found killed in Istanbul May 25.

- May 16 – A coup attempt is exposed and foiled in Egypt.
- May 18
  - The U.S. Congress formally votes to end funding for the American Supersonic Transport program.
  - The Montréal Canadiens win the Stanley Cup against the Chicago Blackhawks. The Canadiens became only the second team in NHL history to win the Cup in game 7 on the road. This also marked the last NHL game that the late Jean Béliveau played.
- May 19 – Mars probe program: *Mars 2* is launched by the Soviet Union.
- May 22 – An earthquake lasting 20 seconds destroys most of Bingöl, Turkey – more than 1,000 are killed, 10,000 made homeless.
- May 23 – An air crash at Rijeka Airport, Yugoslavia kills 78 people, mostly British tourists.
- May 26
  - Austria and the People's Republic of China establish diplomatic relations.
  - Qantas agrees to pay $500,000 to bomb hoaxer-extortionist Mr. Brown (Peter Macari), who is later arrested.
- May 27
  - Six armed passengers hijack a Romanian passenger plane and force it to fly to Vienna.
  - Christie's auctions a diamond known as Deepdene; it is later found to be artificially colored.
- May 28 – Portugal resigns from UNESCO.
- May 30 – Mariner program: *Mariner 9* is launched toward Mars.

- May 31 – The birth of Bangladesh is declared by the government in exile, in territory formerly part of Pakistan.

June

- June – Massachusetts passes its Chapter 766 laws enacting Special Education.
- June 1 – Vietnam War: Vietnam Veterans for a Just Peace, claiming to represent the majority of U.S. veterans who served in Southeast Asia, speak against war protests.
- June 6
  - Soyuz program: *Soyuz 11* (Vladislav Volkov, Georgi Dobrovolski, Viktor Patsayev) is launched.
  - A midair collision between Hughes Airwest Flight 706 Douglas DC-9 jetliner and a U.S. Marine Corps McDonnell Douglas F-4 Phantom jet fighter near Duarte, California, claims 50 lives.
- June 10
  - The U.S. ends its trade embargo of China.
  - Corpus Thursday: A student rally on the streets of Mexico City is roughly dispersed.
- June 11 – Neville Bonner becomes the first Indigenous Australian to sit in the Australian Parliament.
- June 13
  - Vietnam War: *The New York Times* begins to publish the Pentagon Papers.
  - Gijs van Lennep (The Netherlands) and co-driver Helmut Marko (Austria) win the 24 Hours of Le Mans in the Martini Racing Porsche 917K.
- June 14 – Norway begins oil production in the North Sea.

- June 17
    - Representatives of Japan and the United States sign the Okinawa Reversion Agreement, whereby the U.S. will return control of Okinawa.
    - President Richard Nixon declares the U.S. War on Drugs.
- June 18 – Southwest Airlines, a low cost carrier, begins its first flights between Dallas, Houston, and San Antonio.
- June 20 – Britain announces that Soviet space scientist Anatoli Fedoseyev has been granted asylum.
- June 21 – Britain begins new negotiations for EEC membership in Luxembourg.
- June 25 – Madagascar accuses the U.S. of being connected to the plot to oust the current government; the U.S. recalls its ambassador.
- June 27 – Concert promoter Bill Graham closes the legendary Fillmore East, which first opened on 2nd Avenue (between 5th and 6th Streets) in New York City on March 8, 1968.
- June 28 – Assassin Jerome A. Johnson shoots Joe Colombo in the head in a middle of an Italian-American rally, putting him in a coma.
- June 30
    - After a successful mission aboard *Salyut 1*, the world's first manned space station, the crew of the *Soyuz 11* spacecraft are killed when their air supply leaks out through a faulty valve.
    - *New York Times Co. v. United States*: The U.S. Supreme Court rules that the Pentagon Papers may be published, rejecting government injunctions as unconstitutional prior restraint.

July

- July – Nordic Council secretariat inaugurated.
- July 3 – Jim Morrison, lead singer of The Doors is found dead in his bathtub in Paris, France.
- July 4 – Michael S. Hart posts the first e-book, a copy of the United States Declaration of Independence, on the University of Illinois at Urbana–Champaign's mainframe computer, the origin of Project Gutenberg.
- July 5 – Right to vote: The 26th Amendment to the United States Constitution, formally certified by President Richard Nixon, lowers the voting age from 21 to 18.
- July 6 – Hastings Banda is proclaimed President for Life of Malawi.
- July 9 – The United Kingdom increases its troops in Northern Ireland to 11,000.
- July 10–July 11 – Coup attempt in Morocco: 1,400 cadets take over the king's palace for 3 hours and kill 28 people; 158 rebels die when the king's troops storm the palace (10 high-ranking officers are later executed for involvement).
- July 10 – Gloria Steinem makes her Address to the Women of America.
- July 11 – Copper mines in Chile are nationalized.
- July 13
  - Ólafur Jóhannesson forms a government in Iceland.
  - Jordanian army troops launch an offensive against Palestinian guerillas in Jordan.
  - The Yugoslavian government begins allowing foreign companies to take their profits from the country.

- Paced by a prodigious home run by Reggie Jackson, which hits a transformer on the roof of Tiger Stadium, the American League defeats the National League 6-4 in the Major League Baseball All-Star Game in Detroit.
- July 14 – Libya severs its diplomatic ties with Morocco.
- July 15 – American President Richard Nixon announces his 1972 visit to China.
- July 17 – Italy and Austria sign a treaty that ends the schism about South Tyrol.
- July 18 – The Trucial States are formed in the Persian Gulf.
- July 19 – The South Tower of the World Trade Center is topped out at 1,362 feet (415 m), making it the second tallest building in the world.
- July 19–July 23 – Major Hashem al-Atta ousts Jaafar Muhammad al-Nimeiri in a military coup in Sudan. Fighting continues until on July 22, when pro-Nimeiri troops win. Al-Atta and 3 officers are executed.
- July 25–July 30 – Arturo Benedetti Michelangeli records in Munich two Debussy works for Deutsche Grammophon; it's his fifth recording.
- July 26 – *Apollo 15* (carrying astronauts David Scott, Alfred Worden, and James Irwin) is launched.
- July 28 – Abdel Khaliq Mahjub, Sudanese communist leader, is hanged.
- July 29 – The United Kingdom opts out of the Space Race, with the cancellation of its Black Arrow launch vehicle.
- July 30 – In Japan, an All Nippon Airways Boeing 727 collides with a Japanese fighter jet; 162 people are killed.

- July 31 – *Apollo 15* astronauts David Scott and James Irwin become the first to ride in a lunar rover, a day after landing on the Moon.

August

- August – Camden, New Jersey erupts in race riots following the beating death of a Puerto Rican motorist by city police. Looting and arson occurred. This is a turning point in Camden's decline to one of the poorest and highest-crime municipalities in the United States. Camden was, however, the site of a 1949 shooting rampage by Howard Unruh, considered by some to be the first mass murderer in the United States. The riots result in the demise of Camden's Sears and A&P branches. Also in 1971, Philadelphia International Records is established, with Camden native Leon Huff as co-founder.
- August 1 – In New York City, 40,000 attend The Concert for Bangladesh.
- August 2 – J. C. Penney debuts its trademark Helvetica wordmark which has been used ever since.
- August 5 – The South Pacific Forum (SPF) is established.
- August 6 – A lunar eclipse lasting 1 hour, 40 minutes, and 4 seconds is observed.
- August 7 – *Apollo 15* returns to Earth.
- August 9
  - India signs a 20-year treaty of friendship and cooperation with the Soviet Union.
  - Internment in Northern Ireland: British security forces arrest hundreds of nationalists and detain them

without trial in Long Kesh prison; 20 people die in the riots that follow.

- August 11 – Construction begins on the Louisiana Superdome in New Orleans.
- August 12
  - Three thousand people from Belfast and Derry flee to the Republic of Ireland because of the violence.
  - Syria severs diplomatic relations with Jordan because of border clashes.
- August 14
  - British troops are stationed on the Ireland border to stop arms smuggling.
  - Bahrain declares independence as the State of Bahrain (Kingdom of Bahrain as of February 2002).
- August 15
  - Jackie Stewart becomes Formula One World Drivers' Champion in the Tyrrell 003-Cosworth.
  - The number of British troops in Northern Ireland is raised to 12,500.
  - President Richard Nixon announces that the United States will no longer convert dollars to gold at a fixed value, effectively ending the Bretton Woods system. He also imposes a 90-day freeze on wages, prices and rents.
- August 18
  - Vietnam War: Australia and New Zealand decide to withdraw their troops from Vietnam.
  - British troops are engaged in a firefight with the IRA in Derry, Northern Ireland.

- August 19–August 22 – A right-wing coup ignites a rebellion in Bolivia. Miners and students join troops to support president Juan José Torres, but eventually Hugo Banzer takes over.
- August 20
  - International Telecommunications Satellite Organization (Intelsat) (effective 12 February 1973).
  - The USS Manatee (AO-58) spills 1,000 US gallons (3,800 L) of fuel oil on President Nixon's Western White House beach in San Clemente, California.
- August 21 – A bomb made of two hand grenades by communist rebels explodes in the Liberal Party campaign party in Plaza Miranda in Quiapo, Manila the Philippines, injuring several anti-Marcos political candidates.
- August 25
  - Border clashes occur between Tanzania and Uganda.
  - Bangladesh and eastern Bengal are flooded; thousands flee the area.
- August 26 – A civilian government takes power in Greece.
- August 30 – The Progressive Conservatives under Peter Lougheed defeat the Social Credit government under Harry E. Strom in a general election, ending 36 years of uninterrupted power for Social Credit in Alberta.

September

- September – Operation Sourisak Montry VIII opens when forces of the Royal Thai Army recapture several positions in the territory of Laos on the south bank of the Mekong in response to an encroaching Chinese presence to the north.

- September 3
  - Qatar gains independence from the United Kingdom. Unlike most nearby emirates, Qatar declines to become part of either the United Arab Emirates or Saudi Arabia.
  - Manlio Brosio resigns as NATO Secretary General.
- September 4 – A Boeing 727 (Alaska Airlines Flight 1866) crashes into the side of a mountain near Juneau, Alaska, killing all 111 people on board.
- September 8 – In Washington, D.C., the John F. Kennedy Center for the Performing Arts is inaugurated, with the opening feature being the premiere of Leonard Bernstein's *Mass*.
- September 9 – September 13 – Attica Prison riots: – A revolt breaks out at the maximum-security prison in Attica, New York. In the end, state police and the United States National Guard storm the facility; 42 are killed, 10 of them hostages.
- September 19 – Trams in Ballarat (Victoria, Australia) cease to run.
- September 21 – Pakistan declares a state of emergency.
- September 24 – Britain expels 90 KGB and GRU officials; 15 are not allowed to return.
- September 27–October 11 – Japanese Emperor Hirohito travels abroad.
- September 28 – Cardinal József Mindszenty, who has taken refuge in the U.S. Embassy in Budapest since 1956, is allowed to leave Hungary.
- September 29 – A cyclone in the Bay of Bengal, in the Indian state of Odisha, kills 10,000.

October

- October 1 – Walt Disney World opens in Orlando, Florida.
- October 14 – Greenpeace is founded in Vancouver, Canada.
- October 18 – In New York City, the Knapp Commission begins public hearings on police corruption.
- October 21
  - U.S. President Richard Nixon nominates Lewis Franklin Powell, Jr. and William H. Rehnquist to the U.S. Supreme Court.
  - The Clarkston explosion in Scotland kills 22 people.
- October 25 – The United Nations General Assembly admits the People's Republic of China and expels the Republic of China (or Taiwan).
- October 27 – The Democratic Republic of the Congo is renamed Zaire.
- October 28
  - The British House of Commons votes 356–244 in favour of joining the European Economic Community.
  - The United Kingdom becomes the 6th nation to launch a satellite into orbit, the Prospero X-3, using a Black Arrow carrier rocket.
  - The Egyptian Opera House (Khedivial Opera House) burns down in Cairo.
- October 29 – Vietnam War – Vietnamization: The total number of American troops still in Vietnam drops to a record low of 196,700 (the lowest since January 1966).
- October 30 – Rev. Ian Paisley's Democratic Unionist Party is founded in Northern Ireland.

- October 31 – A bomb explodes at the top of the Post Office Tower in London.

November

- November 3 – The UNIX *Programmer's Manual* is published.
- November 6 – Operation Grommet: The U.S. tests a thermonuclear warhead at Amchitka Island in Alaska, code-named Project Cannikin. At around 5 megatons, it is the largest ever U.S. underground detonation.
- November 8 – Led Zeppelin releases their Fourth Studio album "Led Zeppelin IV", which goes on to sell 23,000,000 copies.
- November 9 – A Royal Air Force C-130 crashes into the Ligurian Sea near Leghorn, Italy, killing all 51 people on board.
- November 10 – In Cambodia, Khmer Rouge forces attack Phnom Penh and its airport, killing 44, wounding at least 30 and damaging 9 airplanes.
- November 12 – Vietnam War – Vietnamization: U.S. President Richard M. Nixon sets February 1, 1972, as the deadline for the removal of another 45,000 American troops from Vietnam.
- November 13 – Mariner program: *Mariner 9* becomes the first spacecraft to enter Mars orbit successfully.
- November 14 – Pope Shenouda III of Alexandria is enthroned.
- November 15
  - Intel releases the world's first microprocessor, the Intel 4004.

- International Organization and System of Space Communications (Intersputnik) (effective 12 July 1972).
- November 20 – A bridge still in construction, called Elevado Engenheiro Freyssinet, falls over the Paulo de Frontin Avenue, in Rio de Janeiro, Brazil; 48 people are killed and several injured. Reconstructed, the bridge is currently a part of the Linha Vermelha elevate.
- November 23 – The People's Republic of China takes the Republic of China's seat on the United Nations Security Council (see China and the United Nations).
- November 24
  - During a severe storm over Washington State, a man calling himself D. B. Cooper parachutes from the Northwest Orient Airlines plane he'd just hijacked, with US$200,000 in ransom money, and is never seen again (as of March 2008, this case remains the only unsolved skyjacking in history).
  - A Brussels court sentences pretender Alexis Brimeyer to 18 months in jail for falsely using a noble title; Brimeyer has already fled to Greece.
- November 28 – The 59th Grey Cup Game sees the Calgary Stampeders beat the Toronto Argonauts 14-11.

December

- December 1 – Cambodian Civil War: Khmer Rouge rebels intensify assaults on Cambodian government positions, forcing their retreat from Kompong Thmar and nearby Ba Ray, 10 kilometers northeast of Phnom Penh.

- December 2 – Six Persian Gulf sheikdoms found the United Arab Emirates.
- December 3 – The Indo-Pakistani War of 1971 begins with Operation Chengiz Khan as Pakistan launches preemptive attacks on nine Indian airbases. The next day India launches a massive invasion of East Pakistan.
- December 3–4 – The Pakistani submarine PNS *Ghazi* (former USS *Diablo*) sinks mysteriously near the Indian coast while laying mines.
- December 4
  - The Montreux Casino burns down during a Frank Zappa concert (the event is memorialized in the Deep Purple song "Smoke on the Water"). The casino is rebuilt in 1975.
  - The McGurk's Bar bombing by the Ulster Volunteer Force in Belfast kills 15.
- December 8 – U.S. President Richard Nixon orders the 7th Fleet to move towards the Bay of Bengal in the Indian Ocean.
- December 10 – The John Sinclair Freedom Rally in support of the imprisoned activist features a performance by John Lennon at Crisler Arena, Ann Arbor, Michigan.
- December 11 – Nihat Erim forms the new government of Turkey (34th government; Nihat Erim has served two times as prime minister).
- December 16 – *Victory Day of Bangladesh*: The Pakistan Army in East Pakistan (now Bangladesh) surrenders to the freedom fighters of Bangladesh, ending the Bangladesh Liberation War.
- December 18

- o The U.S. dollar is devalued for the second time in history.
- o The world's largest hydroelectric plant in Krasnoyarsk, Soviet Union, begins operations.
- December 19
  - o Clube Atlético Mineiro wins the Brazil Football Championship.
  - o Intelsat IV (F3) is launched; it enters commercial service over the Atlantic Ocean February 18, 1972.
  - o The controversial dystopian crime film *A Clockwork Orange* directed by Stanley Kubrick is released in New York City.
- December 24
  - o Giovanni Leone is elected President of the Italian Republic.
  - o Juliane Koepcke survives a fall of 10,000 feet following disintegration of LANSA Flight 508.
- December 25
  - o In the longest American football game in National Football League history, the Miami Dolphins beat the Kansas City Chiefs.
  - o A fire at a 22-story hotel in Seoul, South Korea kills 158 people.
- December 29 – The United Kingdom gives up its military bases in Malta.

Date unknown

- Ray Tomlinson sends the first ARPANET e-mail between host computers.
- The Free State of Christiania is founded.
- Seychelles International Airport in Victoria, Seychelles (Mahe) is completed.
- Crude oil production peaks in the continental United States at approximately 4.5 million barrels per day (720,000 m³/d).
- The Center for Science in the Public Interest is established.
- The National Institute on Alcohol Abuse and Alcoholism is established.
- The British crime magazine *Master Detective*, in an attempt to capitalize on the murder of Diane Maxwell, illegally takes photo negatives from Houston, Texas and uses them for a 1971 edition.
- Kamuzu Banda, president of Malawi, becomes the first Black President to visit South Africa.

Births

January

Jeremy Renner

Pep Guardiola

Lee Young-ae

- January 1
    - Sammie Henson, American wrestler, Olympic silver medalist
    - Bridget Pettis, American basketball player
- January 2
    - Lisa Harrison, American basketball player
    - Taye Diggs, African-American actor
- January 3 – Cory Cross, Canadian ice hockey player
- January 5 – Mayuko Takata, Japanese actress
- January 7
    - DJ Ötzi, Austrian entertainer and singer
    - Jeremy Renner, American actor, singer and producer
- January 9 – Scott Thornton, Canadian hockey player
- January 11 – Mary J. Blige, African-American singer

- January 12 – Jay Burridge, British artist and television presenter
- January 13 – Matt McIntosh, American rock singer
- January 14 – Lasse Kjus, Norwegian alpine skier
- January 15 – Regina King, African-American actress
- January 17 – Kid Rock, American rock singer
- January 18
  - Pep Guardiola, Spanish football manager
  - Fabian Ribauw, Nauruan politician
  - Jonathan Davis, American musician (Korn)
- January 20 – Gary Barlow, British singer-songwriter
- January 21 – Alan McManus, Scottish snooker player
- January 25 – Luca Badoer, Italian race car driver
- January 26 – Li Ming, Chinese footballer and football executive
- January 27
  - Fann Wong, Singaporean Chinese actress, model, and singer
  - Lil Jon, American rapper and producer
- January 29 – Clare Balding, British sports presenter
- January 30 – Lizzie Grubman, American publicist
- January 31
  - Lee Young-ae, South Korean actress
  - Patrick "Pat" Kielty, Northern Irish comedian and television presenter
  - Patricia Velásquez, Venezuelan actress and model

February

Michael C. Hall

Daniel Powter

Gillian Flynn

Denise Richards

- February 1 – Michael C. Hall, American actor
- February 2 – Andrus Veerpalu, Estonian cross-country skier
- February 3 – Sarah Kane, English playwright (d. 1999)
- February 4 – Fatmir Limaj, Albanian politician
- February 9 – Sharon Case, American model and actress
- February 10
  - Lisa Marie Varon, American professional wrestler
  - Lorena Rojas, Mexican actress (d. 2015)
- February 11 – Damian Lewis, English actor and producer
- February 13 – Mats Sundin, Swedish ice hockey player
- February 14
  - Kris Aquino, Filipina actress
  - Tommy Dreamer, American professional wrestler
  - Nelson Frazier, Jr., American professional wrestler (d. 2014)
- February 15 – Renee O'Connor, American actress
- February 16 – Amanda Holden, British actress
- February 17 – Denise Richards, American actress
- February 18 – Thomas Bjørn, Danish golfer
- February 19 – Gil Shaham, Israeli/American violinist
- February 20

- ○ Calpernia Addams, American actress
- ○ Jari Litmanen, Finnish footballer
- February 23 – Melinda Messenger, English television presenter
- February 24
  - ○ Pedro de la Rosa, Spanish Formula One driver
  - ○ Gillian Flynn, American author, comic book writer, and screenwriter
- February 25
  - ○ Sean Astin, American actor
  - ○ Daniel Powter, Canadian singer
- February 26 – Max Martin, Swedish music producer and songwriter
- February 27 – Rozonda Thomas, African-American singer
- February 28 – Tristan Louis, French Internet entrepreneur

March

Peter Sarsgaard

Johnny Knoxville

Jon Hamm

Nathan Fillion

Ewan McGregor

- March 2
  - Method Man, African-American rapper, record producer, and actor
  - Roman Čechmánek, Czech hockey goalie
  - Manami Toyota, Japanese professional wrestler
- March 4
  - Iain Baird, Canadian soccer player
  - Shavar Ross, American actor and filmmaker
- March 5 – Yuri Lowenthal, American voice actor
- March 6 – Val Venis, American professional wrestler
- March 7 – Peter Sarsgaard, American actor
- March 9 – Kinga Rusin, Polish journalist
- March 10 – Jon Hamm, American actor, director and producer
- March 11 – Johnny Knoxville, American actor
- March 16 – Alan Tudyk, American actor
- March 22
  - Iben Hjejle, Danish actress
  - Will Yun Lee, Korean-American actor
- March 23
  - Karen McDougal, American model
  - Alexander Selivanov, Russian ice hockey player
- March 26 – Behzad Ghorbani, Iranian scientist
- March 27
  - David Coulthard, Scottish racing driver
  - Nathan Fillion, Canadian actor
- March 29
  - Attila Csihar, Hungarian vocalist
  - Robert Gibbs, White House Press Secretary
- March 31

- Pavel Bure, Russian ice hockey player
- Craig McCracken, American animator
- Ewan McGregor, Scottish actor

April

David Tennant

- April 1 – Jessica Collins, American actress
- April 2
  - Todd Woodbridge, Australian tennis player
  - Zeebra, Japanese rapper
- April 3 – Picabo Street, American skier
- April 9 – Jacques Villeneuve, Canadian Formula 1 race driver
- April 11 – Oliver Riedel, German musician (Rammstein)
- April 12 – Shannen Doherty, American actress
- April 16
  - Peter Billingsley, American actor, director and producer
  - Moses Chan, Hong Kong actor
  - Selena Quintanilla-Pérez, Mexican-American singer (d. 1995)
- April 18 – David Tennant, Scottish actor

- April 19
  - Scott McCord, Canadian voice actor
  - Wendy Powell, American voice actress
- April 20
  - Carla Geurts, Dutch swimmer
  - Allan Houston, American basketball player
  - Mikey Welsh, American musician and artist (d. 2011)
- April 22 – Daisuke Enomoto, first Japanese space tourist
- April 29
  - Tamara Johnson-George, African-American singer (SWV)
  - Siniša Vuco, Croatian musician
- April 30 – John Boyne, Irish novelist

May

Paul Bettany

Idina Menzel

- May 1
  - Stuart Appleby, Australian golfer
  - Ajith Kumar, Indian film actor
- May 8 – Ross Anderson, American pro speed skier
- May 12 – Doug Basham, American professional wrestler
- May 14 – Sofia Coppola, American filmmaker
- May 15 – Phil Pfister, American strength athlete
- May 17
  - Vernie Bennett, English singer (Eternal)
  - Queen Máxima of the Netherlands
- May 19 – Peter Boström, Swedish music producer and songwriter, co-writer of Euphoria
- May 20 – Tony Stewart, American race car driver
- May 25 – Kristina Orbakaitė, Lithuanian-Russian singer and actress
- May 26 – Matt Stone, American actor and producer
- May 27
  - Mathew Batsiua, Nauruan politician
  - Paul Bettany, British actor
  - Wayne Carey, Australian rules footballer
  - Lisa Lopes, African-American rapper (TLC) (d. 2002)
- May 28 – Marco Rubio, U.S Senator from Florida since 2011
- May 30 – Idina Menzel, American singer, songwriter and actress

June

Noah Wyle

Mark Wahlberg

Elon Musk

- June 1 – Mario Cimarro, Cuban actor and singer

- June 4
  - Joseph Kabila, President of the Democratic Republic of the Congo
  - Noah Wyle, American actor
- June 5
  - Susan Lynch, Northern Irish actress
  - Mark Wahlberg, American actor, producer, businessman, model and rapper
- June 8
  - Jeff Douglas, Canadian actor
  - Troy Vincent, American football player
- June 10
  - Bobby Jindal, American Governor of Louisiana
  - Kyle Sandilands, Australian DJ, *Australian Idol* judge and TV presenter
- June 11 – Kenjiro Tsuda, Japanese voice actor
- June 12
  - Arman Alizad, Finnish tailor, columnist and TV personality
  - Mark Henry, American professional wrestler, former Olympian
- June 15 – Isménia do Frederico, Cape Verdean sprinter
- June 16 – Tupac Shakur, African-American rapper and actor (d. 1996)
- June 17 – Paulina Rubio, Mexican singer
- June 18 – Nathan Morris, African-American singer (Boyz II Men)
- June 20 – Josh Lucas, American actor
- June 21 – Anette Olzon, Swedish singer (Nightwish)
- June 22 – Kurt Warner, former American football player

- June 25
  - Neil Lennon, Northern Irish footballer
  - Scott Maslen, English actor
- June 26 – Max Biaggi, Italian motercycle racer
- June 27
  - King Dipendra of Nepal (d. 2001)
  - Kieren Keke, Nauruan politician
- June 28
  - Abu Bakr al-Baghdadi, Iraqi Islamic extremist leader
  - Fabien Barthez, French football player
  - Norika Fujiwara, Japanese actress and television personality
  - Akiko Kimura, Japanese voice actress
  - Aileen Quinn, American actress
  - Elon Musk, South African-born, Canadian-American entrepreneur, engineer, inventor and investor
- June 29
  - Matthew Good, Canadian musician
  - Junko Noda, Japanese voice actress
- June 30 – Jamie McLennan, retired professional ice hockey goaltender, radio sports analyst

July

Julian Assange

Vitali Klitschko

Sandra Oh

- July 1
  - Amira Casar, French actress
  - Missy "Misdemeanor" Elliott, African-American rapper, singer, and songwriter
- July 3 – Julian Assange, Australian activist
- July 9
  - Marc Andreessen, American software developer
  - Scott Grimes, American actor
- July 11 – Brett Hauer, American ice hockey player
- July 12
  - Robert Allenby, Australian golfer
  - Kristi Yamaguchi, American figure skater
- July 13 – Craig Elliott, American illustrator
- July 14
  - Alison Bartlett-O'Reilly, American actress

- o Mark LoMonaco, American professional wrestler
- o Joey Styles, American professional wrestling announcer
- o Howard Webb, English referee
- July 16 – Corey Feldman, American actor
- July 17 – Cory Doctorow, Canadian author and activist
- July 18 – Penny Hardaway, American basketball player
- July 19 – Vitali Klitschko, Ukrainian boxer
- July 20 – Sandra Oh, Korean-Canadian actress
- July 20 – DJ Screw, African-American hip hop DJ (d. 2000)
- July 21
  - o Charlotte Gainsbourg, French actress and singer-songwriter
  - o Nuno Markl, Portuguese comedian and radio host
- July 23
  - o Ahmed Ezz, Egyptian actor
  - o Alison Krauss, American country singer
  - o Scott Krippayne, American Christian musician
- July 26 – Khaled Mahmud, Bangladeshi cricketer
- July 28 – Jeffrey S. Williams, American sportswriter
- July 30 – Tom Green, Canadian entertainer

August

Jeff Gordon

Justin Theroux

Richard Armitage

Carla Gugino

- August 2 – Michael Hughes, Northern Irish footballer
- August 4
  - Jeff Gordon, American race car driver
  - Yo-Yo, African-American rapper
- August 8 – Ali Liebegott, American author and poet
- August 10
  - Roy Keane, Irish footballer

- Mario César Kindelán Mesa, Cuban amateur boxer
- Justin Theroux, American actor
- August 12
  - Patrick Carpentier, Canadian race car driver
  - Pete Sampras, American tennis player
  - Phil Western, Canadian musician
- August 13
  - Moritz Bleibtreu, German actor
  - Heike Makatsch, German actress
- August 17
  - Anthony Kearns, Irish tenor
  - Jorge Posada, Puerto Rican baseball player
- August 19 – Guido Cantz, German television presenter
- August 20 – David Walliams, English comedy actor
- August 21 – Robert Harvey, Australian rules footballer
- August 22
  - Richard Armitage, English actor
  - Benoît Violier, French-born chef (suicide 2016)
- August 25 – Ayumi Miyazaki, Japanese singer
- August 26
  - Gaynor Faye, British actress
  - Thalía, Mexican actress and singer
- August 27 – Julian Cheung, Hong Kong actor and singer
- August 28 – Janet Evans, American swimmer
  - Daniel Goddard, Australian actor and model
- August 29 – Carla Gugino, American actress
- August 31
  - Pádraig Harrington, Irish golfer
  - Chris Tucker, American actor and comedian

September

David Arquette

Martin Freeman

Amy Poehler

Jada Pinkett Smith

Alfonso Ribeiro

- September 1 – Hakan Şükür, Turkish footballer
- September 2
  - Kjetil André Aamodt, Norwegian alpine skier
  - Arnold Arre, Filipino graphic novelist
  - Tommy Maddox, American football player
  - Shauna Sand, American model and actress
- September 4 – Anita Yuen, Hong Kong actress
- September 6 – Dolores O'Riordan, Irish singer
- September 8
  - David Arquette, American actor
  - Brooke Burke-Charvet, American model
  - Martin Freeman, English actor

- September 9
  - Eric Stonestreet, American actor
  - Henry Thomas, American actor
- September 13 – Stella McCartney, British fashion designer, daughter of Paul McCartney
- September 15 – Colleen O'Shaughnessey, American voice actress
- September 16 – Amy Poehler, American actress
- September 17 – Jens Voigt, German cyclist
- September 18
  - Lance Armstrong, American cyclist
  - Anna Netrebko, Russian operatic soprano
  - Jada Pinkett Smith, African-American actress
- September 19 – Sanaa Lathan, African-American actress
- September 20 – Henrik Larsson, Swedish footballer
- September 21
  - Luke Wilson, American actor
  - Alfonso Ribeiro, American actor, television director, dancer, and current host of America's Funniest Home Videos
- September 22
  - Chesney Hawkes, English singer-songwriter
  - Ted Leonard, American singer (Enchant)
- September 23 – Lee Mi-yeon, South Korean actress
- September 24 – Michael S. Engel, American paleontologist and entomologist
- September 25 – Jessie Wallace, English actress
- September 27 – Horacio Sandoval, Mexican artist
- September 29 – Sibel Tüzün, Turkish pop/rock/jazz singer
- September 30

- Jenna Elfman, American actress
- Jeff Whitty, American playwright

October

Sacha Baron Cohen

Snoop Dogg

Winona Ryder

- October 2
  - Xavier Naidoo, German singer
  - Tiffany, American singer

- October 3 – Kevin Richardson, American pop singer (Backstreet Boys)
- October 5 – Samuel Vincent, Canadian voice actor
- October 10
  - Tiffany Mynx, American porn actress and director
  - Evgeny Kissin, Russian pianist
- October 12 _ Đàm Vĩnh Hưng,Vietnamese singer
- October 13
  - Sacha Baron Cohen, English comedian and actor
  - Pyrros Dimas, Greek weightlifter
- October 14
  - Andy Cole, English Footballer
  - Jorge Costa, Portuguese footballer
- October 16 – Mirko Reisser (DAIM), German graffiti-artist
- October 17 – Chris Kirkpatrick, American singer ('N Sync)
- October 20
  - Snoop Dogg, African-American rapper
  - Dannii Minogue, Australian singer
- October 21 – Jade Jagger, English jewelry designer
- October 23 – Bohuslav Sobotka, Prime Minister of the Czech Republic
- October 24 – Caprice Bourret, American model and actress
- October 25
  - Athena Chu, Hong Kong actress and singer
  - Midori Gotō, Japanese violinist
  - Pedro Martínez, Dominican baseball player
- October 29 – Winona Ryder, American actress

November

Tech N9ne

David DeLuise

Christina Applegate

Michael Strahan

- November 3 – Dylan Moran, Irish comedian, actor, and writer
- November 4 – Tabu, Indian actress
- November 5 – Jonny Greenwood, English musician and composer
- November 7
  - Robin Finck, American guitarist (Nine Inch Nails, Guns N' Roses)
  - Rituparna Sengupta, Indian film actress
- November 8
  - Carlos Atanes, Spanish film director
  - Tech N9ne, American rapper
- November 10
  - Big Pun, American/Latin rapper (d. 2000)
  - Niki Karimi, Iranian actress and movie director
- November 11 – David DeLuise, American actor
- November 12 – Yasuo Aiuchi, Japanese snowboarder
- November 12 – Chen Guangcheng, Chinese civil rights activist
- November 14
  - Adam Gilchrist, Australian cricketer
  - Marco Leonardi, Italian actor
- November 16 – Alexander Popov, Russian swimmer
- November 17 – Michael Adams, British chess player
- November 18 – Özlem Tekin, Turkish singer
- November 19 – Sundeep Malani, Indian film director
- November 20
  - Dion Nash, New Zealand cricket captain
  - Joel McHale, American actor

- November 21 – Michael Strahan, Television host and retired American football player
- November 22 – Kyran Bracken, English rugby player
- November 23 – Chris Hardwick, American actor and comedian
- November 24 – Keith Primeau, Canadian hockey player
- November 25
  - Christina Applegate, American actress
  - Magnus Arvedson, Swedish hockey player
- November 30
  - Iván "Pudge" Rodríguez, Puerto Rican baseball player and actor
  - Jessalyn Gilsig, Canadian actress

December

Ricky Martin

Giorgos Alkaios

Jared Leto

Justin Trudeau

- December 1 – Jason Keng-Kwin Chan, Malaysian-Australian actor
- December 2 – Mine Yoshizaki, Japanese manga artist
- December 5 – Kali Rocha, American actress
- December 6
  - Helena Bulaja, Croatian multimedia artist
  - Richard Krajicek, Dutch tennis player
- December 7
  - Vladimir Akopian, Armenian chess player
  - Larisa Alexandrovna, Ukrainian-American feminist
- December 8 – Abdullah Ercan, Turkish football player

- December 10 – Michele Mahone, American television entertainment reporter and former make-up artist and hair stylist
- December 12 – Sammy Korir, Kenyan long-distance runner
- December 15 – Arne Quinze, Belgian conceptual artist
- December 16
    - Michael McCary, African-American singer (Boyz II Men)
    - Paul van Dyk, German dance music DJ, musician and record producer
- December 17
    - Antoine Rigaudeau, French basketball player
    - Alan Khan, South African radio DJ
    - Sinan Akkuş, Turkish-German actor
- December 18
    - Jason Hughes, Welsh actor
    - Arantxa Sánchez Vicario, Spanish tennis player
- December 20 – Simon O'Neill, New Zealand opera singer
- December 22 – Khalid Khannouchi, Moroccan long-distance runner
- December 23
    - Corey Haim, Canadian actor (d. 2010)
    - Tara Palmer-Tomkinson, British socialite
- December 24
    - Giorgos Alkaios, Greek recording artist
    - Christopher Daniels, American professional wrestler
    - Ricky Martin, Puerto Rican singer
- December 25
    - Dido, English singer
    - Justin Trudeau, 23rd Prime Minister of Canada

- December 26 – Jared Leto, American actor and musician
- December 31 – Brent Barry, American basketball player

Date unknown

- Vic Pratt, English writer

Deaths

January

Coco Chanel

- January 4 – Arthur Ford, American psychic spiritual medium, clairaudient (b. 1896)
- January 5 – Douglas Shearer, Canadian film sound engineer (b. 1899)
- January 9 – Elmer Flick, American baseball player (Cleveland Indians) and a member of the MLB Hall of Fame (b. 1876)
- January 10 – Coco Chanel, French fashion designer (b. 1883)
- January 12 – John Tovey, British admiral (b. 1885)
- January 14 – Guillermo de Torre, Spanish Dadaist author (b. 1900)

- January 15 – John Dall, American actor (b. 1918)
- January 20 – Gilbert M. 'Broncho Billy' Anderson, American actor, director, writer, and producer (b. 1880)
- January 23 – Fritz Feigl, Austria-born chemist (b. 1875)
- January 24
  - St. John Greer Ervine, Northern Irish dramatist and author (b. 1883)
  - Bill W. (William Griffith Wilson), co-founder Alcoholics Anonymous (b. 1895)
- January 25
  - Barry III, Guinean politician (b. 1923)
  - Hermann Hoth, German general (b. 1885)
  - Isobel Lennart, American screenwriter (b. 1915)
- January 27 – Jacobo Árbenz, President of Guatemala (b. 1913)
- January 28 – Donald Winnicott, British psychoanalyst (b. 1896)
- January 31 – Viktor Maksimovich Zhirmunsky, Russian literary historian, linguist (b. 1891)

February

- February 1 – Robert Gordon, American actor (b. 1895)
- February 2 – Secundino Zuazo, Spanish architect and city planner (b. 1887)
- February 3 – Jay C. Flippen, American actor (b. 1899)
- February 4 – Charles Lahr, German-born anarchist, London bookseller and publisher (b. 1885)
- February 5 – Samuel Fox, American music publisher and founder of the Sam Fox Publishing Company (b. 1884)

- February 8 – Charles Walter Simpson, English painter (b. 1885)
- February 12 – James Cash Penney, American founder of J. C. Penney (b. 1875)
- February 13 – Emil Fuchs, German theologian (b. 1874)
- February 18 – Jaime de Barros Câmara, Brazilian archbishop (b. 1894)
- February 19 – Edwin North McClellan, United States Marine Corps (b. 1881)
- February 22 – William B. Hartsfield, American politician (b. 1890)
- February 25 – Theodor Svedberg, Swedish chemist, Nobel Prize laureate (b. 1884)
- February 26 – Yahei Miura, Japanese athlete (b. 1895)

March

- March 5 – Jean Grenier, French philosopher and writer (b. 1898)
- March 6 – Herbert McLean Evans, U.S. anatomist and embryologist (b. 1882)
- March 7 – Barney Balaban, American studio executive (b. 1887)
- March 8
  - Borden Chase, American screenwriter (b. 1900)
  - Harold Lloyd, American actor and filmmaker (b. 1893)
  - James Tait Plowden-Wardlaw, Vicar of St Clement's Cambridge and a barrister (b. 1873)
- March 9 – Pope Cyril VI of Alexandria, Coptic Orthodox Patriarch (b. 1902)

- March 11
  - Philo T. Farnsworth, American television pioneer (b. 1906)
  - C. D. Broad, English philosopher (b. 1887)
- March 12 – David Burns, American actor (b. 1902)
- March 16
  - Bebe Daniels, American actress (b. 1901)
  - Thomas E. Dewey, Governor of New York; American presidential candidate (b. 1902)
- March 17 – Elizabeth Okie Paxton, American painter (b. 1877)
- March 18 – Leland Hayward, American film and theatrical agent (b. 1902)
- March 19 – Winifred Horrabin, British socialist activist and journalist (b. 1887)
- March 23 – Basil Dearden, English film director (b. 1911)
- March 24
  - Arne Jacobsen, Danish architect and designer (b. 1902)
  - Arthur Metcalfe, Australian public servant (b. 1895)
- March 31 – Karl King, United States march music (b. 1891)

April

Igor Stravinsky

- April 1 – Ramiro Arrue, Basque painter, illustrator, and ceramist (b. 1892)
- April 3 – Joseph Valachi, American gangster (b. 1904)
- April 6
    - Igor Stravinsky, Russian composer (b. 1882)
    - Margaret Newton, Canadian plant pathologist and mycologist (b. 1887)
- April 8 – Ivan Vurnik, Slovene architect that helped found the Ljubljana School of Architecture (b. 1884)
- April 12 – Igor Tamm, Russian physicist, Nobel Prize laureate (b. 1895)
- April 13 – Juhan Smuul, Estonian writer (b. 1922)
- April 15 – Friedebert Tuglas, Estonian writer and critic (b. 1886)
- April 16 – William Eckert, Commissioner of American baseball (b. 1909)
- April 17 – William Corbett, American attorney, acting Governor of Guam (b. 1902)
- April 19 – Earl Thomson, Canadian athlete (b. 1895)
- April 20 – Cecil Parker, English actor (b. 1897)
- April 21
    - Papa Doc Duvalier, President of Haiti (b. 1907)
    - Edmund Lowe, American actor (b. 1890)
- April 26 – T. V. Soong, Republic of China businessman and politician (b. 1891)
- April 29 – Nikolai P. Barabashov, Russian astronomer (b.1894)

May

- May 1
  - Glenda Farrell, American actress (b. 1904)
  - Cheridah de Beauvoir Stocks, the second British woman to gain a Royal Aero Club aviator licence, in 1911 (b. 1887)
- May 2 – Semaun, first chairman of the Communist Party (b. 1899)
- May 11 – Seán Lemass, Taoiseach of Ireland (b. 1899)
- May 12
  - Harold Lea Fetherstonhaugh, Canadian architect from Montreal, Quebec (b. 1887)
  - Tor Johnson, Swedish wrestler and actor (b. 1903)
  - Heinie Manush, American baseball player (b. 1901)
- May 15
  - Goose Goslin, American baseball player (b. 1900)
  - Sir Tyrone Guthrie, English film director, producer, and writer (b. 1900)
- May 17 – German cinematographer, Georg Muschner (b. 1885)
- May 18
  - G. Owen Bonawit, stained glass artist (b. 1891)
  - Bruno Villabruna, Italian lawyer and politician (b. 1884)
- May 19
  - Ogden Nash, American poet (b. 1902)
  - Bernard Wagenaar, Dutch/American composer, conductor and violinist (b. 1894)
- May 21 – Dennis King, English actor (b. 1897)

- May 26 – Laurence Wild, American basketball player, coach, and 30th Governor of American Samoa (b. 1890)
- May 27 – Chips Rafferty, Australian actor (b. 1909)
- May 28
    - Eduardo Blanco Acevedo, Uruguayan political figure and physician (b. 1884)
    - Garnet Kearney, Canadian doctor, teacher, and pioneer (b. 1884)
    - Kim Iryeop, Korean writer, journalist, feminist activist, Buddhist nun (b. 1896)
    - Thomas McLaughlin, Irish engineer (b. 1896)
    - Audie Murphy, American World War II hero and actor (b. 1924)
    - Alfred Rose (bishop), the sixth Bishop of Dover in the modern era (b. 1884)
    - Miriam Soljak, New Zealand feminist and communist (b. 1879)
    - Jean Vilar, French stage actor (b. 1912)
- May 30 – Marcel Dupré, French composer (b. 1886)

June

- June 1 – Reinhold Niebuhr, American theologian (b. 1892)
- June 4 – György Lukács, Hungarian Marxist philosopher, aesthetician, literary historian, and critic (b. 1885)
- June 10
    - Virginia True Boardman, American actress (b. 1889)
    - Michael Rennie, English actor (b. 1909)
- June 11 – Ambrose (bandleader), English violinist and bandleader (b. 1896)

- June 14 – Carlos P. Garcia, 8th President of the Philippines (b. 1896)
- June 15
    - Herbert Gundelach, German general during the Second World War (b. 1899)
    - Arthur Kaufmann (artist), German painter, (b. 1888)
    - Wendell Meredith Stanley, American chemist, Nobel Prize laureate (b. 1904)
- June 16 – John Reith, 1st Baron Reith, British broadcasting executive (b. 1889)
- June 18
    - Thomas Gomez, American actor (b. 1905)
    - Libby Holman, American singer and actress (b. 1904)
    - Paul Karrer, Swiss chemist, Nobel Prize laureate (b. 1889)
    - Prajnalok Mahasthavir, scholar, writer and orator (b. 1879)
    - Mildred Veitch, last member of the Veitch family of horticulturists (b. 1889)
- June 25 – John Boyd Orr, Scottish physician and biologist, recipient of the Nobel Peace Prize (b. 1880)
- June 30
    - Herbert Biberman, Jewish-American screenwriter and film director (b. 1900)
    - Alexander Curt Brade, German botanist (b. 1881)
    - Crew of Soyuz 11:
        - Georgy Dobrovolsky (b. 1928)
        - Viktor Patsayev (b. 1933)
        - Vladislav Volkov (b. 1935)
    - Gaston Balande, French painter and illustrator (b. 1880)

July

Louis Armstrong

- July 1
  - William Lawrence Bragg, English physicist, Nobel Prize laureate (b. 1890)
  - Learie Constantine, Baron Constantine, Trinidadian cricketer (b. 1901)
- July 3 – Jim Morrison, American rock singer, songwriter, and poet (b. 1943)
- July 4
  - Maurice Bowra, British critic (b. 1898)
  - August Derleth, American author and anthologist (b. 1909)
  - Thomas C. Hart, American admiral and politician (b. 1877)
- July 6 – Louis Armstrong, African-American jazz trumpeter (b. 1901)
- July 7
  - Claude Gauvreau, Canadian writer (b. 1925)
  - Ub Iwerks, American animator (b. 1901)
- July 10 – George Kenner, German artist (b. 1888)
- July 13 – Joseph J. Clark, American admiral, (b. 1893)
- July 15 – Bill Thompson, American voice actor (b. 1913)
- July 17 – Cliff Edwards, American actor (b. 1895)

- July 19
  - John Jacob Astor, 1st Baron Astor of Hever, British businessman (b. 1886)
  - Harry W. Hill, American admiral (b. 1890)
  - Norman Reilly Raine, American screenwriter (b. 1894)
  - Arsène Roux, French Arabist (b. 1893)
- July 21 – Michael Somogyi, Hungarian-American professor of biochemistry (b. 1883)
- July 22 – W. Ross Thatcher, Premier of Saskatchewan, Canada (1964–1971) (b. 1917)
- July 23 – Van Heflin, American actor (b. 1910)
- July 24
  - Christl Mardayn, German actress (b. 1896)
  - Alan Rawsthorne, British Composer (b. 1905)
- July 25 – Alfred Michael "Chief" Venne, Ojibwa/Chippewa Native American leader (b. 1879)
- July 26 – Diane Arbus, American photographer (b. 1923)
- July 27 – Charlie Tully, Northern Irish footballer (b. 1924)
- July 30 – Kenneth Slessor, Australian poet (b. 1901)

August

- August 2
  - Satyananda Giri, Indian monk and Yukteswar Giri's chief in Dubai,India (b. 1896)
  - John McDermott, American golfer (b. 1891)
- August 3 – Beatrice Kerr, Australian swimmer, diver, and aquatic performer (b. 1887)
- August 4 – E. Barrett Prettyman, United States federal judge (b. 1891)

- August 5 – Royal Rife, American inventor (b. 1888)
- August 10 – Antoine Mostaert, CICM Missionaries (b. 1881)
- August 11 – John Burton Cleland, Australian naturalist, microbiologist, mycologist and ornithologist (b. 1878)
- August 13 – King Curtis, American saxophonist (b. 1934)
- August 15
  - Albrecht Goetze, German-American Hittitologist (b. 1897)
  - Paul Lukas, Hungarian-born American actor (b. 1895)
- August 17 – Horace McMahon, American actor (b. 1906)
- August 20 – Matiur Rahman, Bangladeshi war hero (b. 1945)
- August 24 – Carl Blegen, American archaeologist (b. 1887)
- August 25 – Ted Lewis, American musician and entertainer (b. 1890)
- August 27
  - Margaret Bourke-White, American photographer (b. 1904)
  - Bennett Cerf, American publisher and television personality (b. 1898)
- August 28
  - Geoffrey Lawrence, 1st Baron Oaksey, British Judge during the Nuremberg trials after World War II (b. 1880)
  - Reuvein Margolies, Austrian-Hungarian-born Israeli author and Talmudic scholar (b. 1889)

September

Nikita Khrushchev

- September 5 – George Trafton, American football player (b. 1897)
- September 7 – Spring Byington, American actress (b. 1886)
- September 10 – Pier Angeli, Italian actress (b. 1932)
- September 11
  - Bella Darvi, Polish-born actress (b. 1928)
  - Percy Helton, American film and television actor (b. 1894)
  - Nikita Khrushchev, Soviet leader (b. 1894)
- September 12 – Lin Biao, Chinese defense minister (b. 1907)
- September 17 – Carlos Lamarca, Brazilian military officer turned guerrilla leader (b. 1937)
- September 20 – Giorgos Seferis, Greek writer, Nobel Prize laureate (b. 1900)
- September 21 – Bernardo Houssay, Argentine physiologist, Nobel Prize laureate (b. 1887)
- September 22 – Lilian Bland, British journalist (b. 1878)
- September 23

- James Waddell Alexander II, mathematician and topologist (b. 1888)
  - Billy Gilbert, American actor (b. 1894)
- September 24 – Hedwiga Reicher, German actress (b. 1884)
- September 25 – Hugo Black, American Supreme Court Justice (b. 1886)

October

- October 2 – Jessie Arms Botke, American artist (b. 1883)
  - Richard H. Jackson, four-star admiral (b. 1866)
- October 3 – Leah Baird, American actress (b. 1883)
- October 6 – Debaki Bose, Bengali director, writer, and actor (b. 1898)
- October 7 – Henry Shoemaker Conard, authority on bryophytes and water lilies (b. 1874)
- October 8 – Johanna Bordewijk-Roepman, Dutch composer (b. 1892)
- October 9 – Peter Rindskopf, American civil rights lawyer (b. 1942)
- October 10 – Cyril Burt, British educational psychologist (b. 1883)
- October 11 – Chester Conklin, American comedic actor (b. 1886)
- October 12
  - Dean Acheson, United States Secretary of State (b. 1893)
  - Gene Vincent, American singer (b. 1935)
- October 13
  - Benito Canónico, Venezuelan composer (b. 1894)
  - Hans Ledersteger, Austrian art director (b. 1898)

- October 16
  - Richard Thomas Alexander, American educator and influential education theorist.(b. 1887)
  - Robin Boyd, Australian architect (b. 1919)
- October 19 – Betty Bronson, American actress (b. 1906)
- October 21
  - Raymond Hatton, American actor (b. 1887)
  - Naoya Shiga, Japanese writer (b. 1883)
- October 24 – Carl Ruggles, American composer (b. 1876)
- October 27 – Gustave Baumann, American printmaker and painter (b. 1881)
- October 29
  - Duane Allman, American rock guitarist (b. 1946)
  - Arne Tiselius, Swedish chemist, Nobel Prize laureate (b. 1902)

November

- November 1 – Gertrud von Le Fort,German writer of novels, poems and essays (b. 1876)
- November 2 – Martha Vickers, American actress (b. 1925)
- November 4 – Guillermo León Valencia, President of Colombia (b. 1909)
- November 9 – Maude Fealy, American stage and film actor (b. 1881)
- November 11 – A. P. Herbert, English humorist, novelist, playwright and law reform activist (b. 1890)
  - Walther Kittel, German general during World War II (b. 1887)
- November 16

- Lucien Chopard, French entomologist (b. 1885)
  - Edie Sedgwick, American actress and model (b. 1943)
- November 17
  - Debaki Bose, Indian actor, director and writer (b. 1898)
  - Dame Gladys Cooper, English actress (b. 1888)
- November 22 – József Zakariás, Hungarian soccer player (b. 1924)
- November 25 – Hank Mann, American comedic actor (b. 1888)
- November 26 – James Alberione,Italian Roman Catholic priest (b. 1884)
- November 27 – Joe Guyon, American football player (b. 1892)
- November 29 – Knud Jessen, Danish botanist and quaternary geologist (b. 1884)

December

Jo Cals

- December 1 – Jason Keng-Kwin Chan, Malaysian-Australian actor
- December 2 – E. M. Almedingen, Russian-British novelist, biographer and children's author (b. 1898)

- December 6 – Mathilde Kschessinska, Russian ballerina (b. 1872)
- December 7 – Ferdinand Pecora, American lawyer and judge (b. 1882)
- December 9 – Ralph Bunche, African-American diplomat, recipient of the Nobel Peace Prize (b. 1904)
- December 12
  - Torrance "Torry" Gillick, Scottish footballer (b. 1915)
  - Nikolai Kudryavtsev, Soviet Russian petroleum geologist (b. 1893)
  - Yechezkel Kutscher, Israeli philologist and Hebrew linguist (b. 1909)
  - Alan Morton, Scottish footballer (b. 1893)
  - David Sarnoff, Radio and television pioneer (b. 1891)
- December 13 – Gotthard Heinrici, German general (b. 1886)
- December 15 – Paul Lévy (mathematician), French mathematician (b. 1886)
- December 16 - Pakistan Army surrendered to the allied force of Bangladesh and India ending the Liberation War of Bangladesh.
- December 18
  - Bobby Jones, American golfer (b. 1902)
  - Diana Lynn, American actress (b. 1926)
- December 20
  - Gustavo Bacarisas, Gibraltarian painter (b. 1873)
  - Roy O. Disney, American studio executive (b. 1893)
- December 22 – Godfried Bomans, Dutch writer (b. 1913)
- December 24
  - Dora Altmann, German actress (b. 1881)
  - Maria Koepcke, German ornithologist (b. 1924)

- December 26 – Robert Lowery, American actor (b. 1913)
- December 28 – Max Steiner, Austrian-born film composer (b. 1888)
- December 29 – Stuart Holmes, American actor (b. 1884)
- December 30 – Dorothy Comingore, American actress (b. 1913)
  - Jo Cals, Dutch politician and jurist, Prime Minister of the Netherlands (1965–1966) (b. 1914)
- December 31
  - Pete Duel, American actor (*Alias Smith and Jones*) (b. 1940)
  - Eduardo Zamacois, Spanish novelist (b. 1873)

Date unknown

- Reg Bunn, British artist (b. 1905)

Nobel Prizes

- Physics – Dennis Gabor
- Chemistry – Gerhard Herzberg
- Medicine – Earl W. Sutherland, Jr
- Literature – Pablo Neruda
- Peace – Willy Brandt
- Economics – Simon Kuznets

In the News.

Decimalisation in United Kingdom and Ireland both switch to decimal currency.

Major General Idi Amin takes control of Uganda soon to become one of the worst and most notorious dictators of modern times.

Charles Manson and three of his followers receive the death penalty.

Ibrox disaster in Scotland.

A new stock market index called the Nasdaq debuts.

IRA Bomb Post Office Tower in London.

Mount Etna erupts.

The Walt Disney World Resort opens in Florida.

Mariner 9 becomes the first spacecraft to orbit another planet in November.

Popular Films - Love Story, Summer of '42, Ryan's Daughter, The Owl and the Pussycat.

1971 Calendar.

January 1971
Sun	Mon	Tue	Wed	Thu	Fri	Sat
					1	2
3	4	5	6	7	8	9
10	11	12	13	14	15	16
17	18	19	20	21	22	23
24	25	26	27	28	29	30
31						

February 1971
Sun	Mon	Tue	Wed	Thu	Fri	Sat
	1	2	3	4	5	6
7	8	9	10	11	12	13
14	15	16	17	18	19	20
21	22	23	24	25	26	27
28						

March 1971
Sun	Mon	Tue	Wed	Thu	Fri	Sat
	1	2	3	4	5	6
7	8	9	10	11	12	13
14	15	16	17	18	19	20
21	22	23	24	25	26	27
28	29	30	31			

April 1971
Sun	Mon	Tue	Wed	Thu	Fri	Sat
				1	2	3
4	5	6	7	8	9	10
11	12	13	14	15	16	17
18	19	20	21	22	23	24
25	26	27	28	29	30	

May 1971
Sun	Mon	Tue	Wed	Thu	Fri	Sat
						1
2	3	4	5	6	7	8
9	10	11	12	13	14	15
16	17	18	19	20	21	22
23	24	25	26	27	28	29
30	31					

June 1971
Sun	Mon	Tue	Wed	Thu	Fri	Sat
		1	2	3	4	5
6	7	8	9	10	11	12
13	14	15	16	17	18	19
20	21	22	23	24	25	26
27	28	29	30			

July 1971
Sun	Mon	Tue	Wed	Thu	Fri	Sat
				1	2	3
4	5	6	7	8	9	10
11	12	13	14	15	16	17
18	19	20	21	22	23	24
25	26	27	28	29	30	31

August 1971
Sun	Mon	Tue	Wed	Thu	Fri	Sat
1	2	3	4	5	6	7
8	9	10	11	12	13	14
15	16	17	18	19	20	21
22	23	24	25	26	27	28
29	30	31				

September 1971
Sun	Mon	Tue	Wed	Thu	Fri	Sat
			1	2	3	4
5	6	7	8	9	10	11
12	13	14	15	16	17	18
19	20	21	22	23	24	25
26	27	28	29	30		

October 1971
Sun	Mon	Tue	Wed	Thu	Fri	Sat
					1	2
3	4	5	6	7	8	9
10	11	12	13	14	15	16
17	18	19	20	21	22	23
24	25	26	27	28	29	30
31						

November 1971
Sun	Mon	Tue	Wed	Thu	Fri	Sat
	1	2	3	4	5	6
7	8	9	10	11	12	13
14	15	16	17	18	19	20
21	22	23	24	25	26	27
28	29	30				

December 1971
Sun	Mon	Tue	Wed	Thu	Fri	Sat
			1	2	3	4
5	6	7	8	9	10	11
12	13	14	15	16	17	18
19	20	21	22	23	24	25
26	27	28	29	30	31